Page and Graphic Designs by Written By Sha, LLC

ISBN: 978-0-692-14586-9

This journal is dedicated to my sons and my husband whom I love so much. Everything I do in life is for you. I fight for you daily.

This journal belongs to:

___

___

If found, please contact me:

___

___

Let's set some G.O.A.L.S. because,
Godly Order Allows Lasting Success!

This part is very important and you shouldn't rush through it! Take some time to flip back to this page at the beginning of each month and set a new goal.

Cheers to growth, healing, love, and forgiveness!

My goal for **January** is to ______________________________

____

My goal for **February** is to ______________________________

____

My goal for **March** is to ______________________________

____

My goal for **April** is to ______________________________

____

My goal for **May** is to ______________________________

____

My goal for **June** is to ______________________________

____

My goal for **July** is to ______________________________

____

My goal for **August** is to ______________________________

____

My goal for **September** is to

My goal for **October** is to

My goal for **November** is to

My goal for **December** is to

And the peace of God, which
transcends all understanding, will
guard your hearts and your minds in
Christ Jesus.
Phillippians 4:7 NIV

What this verse means to me is

My faith was challenged today by

Now faith is confidence in what we hope for and as surance about what we do not see.
Hebrews 11:1 NIV

What this verse means to me is

I pray for healing for

He said to her, "Daughter, your faith has healed you.
Go in peace and be freed from your suffering."
Mark 5:34 NIV

What this verse means to me

Lord, please heal my heart from

For he wounds, but he also binds up; he injures,
but his hands also heal.
Job 5:18 NIV

Today I will forgive someone whom I feel I shouldn't because

Who forgives all your sins and heals all your diseases
Psalm 103:3 NIV

What this verse means to me is

I will forgive daily because

Be kind and compassionate to one another, forgiving each other, just as in Christ God forgave you.
Ephesians 4:32 NIV

What this verse means to me is

"For I know the plans I have for you," declares the lord,
"plans to prosper you and not to harm you,
plans to give you HOPE and a future."
Jeremiah 29:11 NIV

What this verse means to me is

I know that I am capable of complete healing because

Then Jesus said to him, "Get up! Pick up your mat and walk."
John 5:8 NIV

And the peace of God, which
transcends all understanding, will
guard your hearts and your minds in
Christ Jesus.
Phillippians 4:7 NIV

What this verse means to me is

My faith was challenged today by

Now faith is confidence in what we hope for and as surance about what we do not see.
Hebrews 11:1 NIV

What this verse means to me is

I pray for healing for

He said to her, "Daughter, your faith has healed you.
Go in peace and be freed from your suffering."
Mark 5:34 NIV

What this verse means to me

Lord, please heal my heart from

For he wounds, but he also binds up; he injures,
but his hands also heal.
Job 5:18 NIV

Today I will forgive someone whom I feel I shouldn't because

Who forgives all your sins and heals all your diseases
Psalm 103:3 NIV

What this verse means to me is

will forgive daily because

Be kind and compassionate to one another, forgiving each other, just as in Christ God forgave you.
Ephesians 4:32 NIV

What this verse means to me is

"For I know the plans I have for you," declares the lord,
"plans to prosper you and not to harm you,
plans to give you HOPE and a future."
Jeremiah 29:11 NIV

What this verse means to me is

I know that I am capable of complete healing because

Then Jesus said to him, "Get up! Pick up your
mat and walk."
John 5:8 NIV

www.ingramcontent.com/pod-product-compliance
Lightning Source LLC
Chambersburg PA
CBHW070014140726
47908CB00020B/1283

* 9 7 8 0 6 9 2 1 4 5 8 6 9 *